# FLY HEALTHY!

## THE ONLY WAY TO FLY.

## THE JETSETTER HEALTH HANDBOOK

Katharine Clark, RN

ISBN-13: 978-1985694934

ISBN-10: 198569493X

Thank you so much to my friends who helped. I can't mention all of them here. You know who you are.

I do want to Thank:

Jan Smith, who did the editing three times on the final and is my biggest supporter, to finish the book, and in sharing the book.

Karen Ranzi, who pre-read the book and gave me so much encouragement and an early endorsement and then interviewed me in her summit. (superhealthychildren.com)

Barbara Swanson, author of Beyond Food, The Handbook of Function Nutrition who did an early pre-read and edit.

Nonnie Crystal, (healthgems.com) who went through it with a fine tooth comb and checked content and made suggestions.

Dr Gabriel Cousens, who read the draft and gave me an endorsement and of course he has a wonderful section on the subject in his book: Rainbow Green Live Food Cuisine. (treeoflifecenterus.com)

Thank you to all my friends who encouraged me, send information or read the book.

Thank you to every one who has purchased the book, shared the book, and made a review on Amazon, too.

Please remember to put your review of the book on amazon.com after reading it!

# FLY HEALTHY,
# The Only Way to Fly!

## THE JETSETTER HEALTH HANDBOOK
### Katharine Clark, RN
### "The Happy Healthy Jetsetter"

# TABLE OF CONTENTS

# INTRODUCTION

**The World Health Organization says** air travel, particularly over long distances, exposes passengers to a number of factors that may have an effect on their health and well-being. Health risks associated with air travel can be minimized if the traveler plans carefully and takes some simple precautions before, during and after the flight.[26]

I like to make a comfortable cocoon around myself when flying. A few of my friends were curious and asked me to make a list of the simple precautions I take to mitigate the considerable health hazards of jetsetting, I had no idea it would become this book!

I have a lot experience with air travel. I've circumnavigated the planet three times in my life. There were years that involved traveling 34 weekends out of 52, putting me in the million miles club! I continue to learn how to prepare so I arrive healthy and happy. I'd like you to be a healthy happy jetsetter too!

Flying at 30,000 feet at over 500 miles per hour is one of the more stressful things you can do to yourself. Happily, there are ways to minimize the damage. Stress, poor air quality, immobility, radiation exposure, ozone toxicity, inadequate hydration and time zone disruption can all make you more vulnerable to becoming ill immediately or later. These risks increase the more you fly, and most have cumulative effects. For instance, Aerotoxic Association (aerotoxic.org) estimates that over 196,000 passengers a year go to their doctor resulting from discomforts after a flight.

I want to arm you, not alarm you. We know that the body is a self-healing organism. Our bodies have evolved mechanisms for dealing with stressors. Radiation, toxins, fatigue, and irritations are not new to our gene pool. Bad bugs, germs, viruses and other pathogens in general, are not new to the human race. Today we are faced with relatively new pathogens like MRSA and a multitude of viruses. Our bodies have adapted successful strategies for eliminating toxins, resisting stress, and withstanding radiation. IN this book, I'm going to share effective strategies for minimizing the effect of these stressors on your health.

What we face while in an airport and in the airplane are extremes of several stressors. Some have cumulative effects, and many of them are stressing us simultaneously. In terms of pathogens, you'll be exposed to an international blend of opportunistic jetsetting pathogens!

It is smart to take steps to support your health and well-being during air travel so you can enjoy its benefits. Many of my suggestions are good strategies for staying healthy even on the ground, so adopting some of these new habits might help you make overall improvements in your lifestyle choices.

My strategy is to enjoy the benefits of travel, while avoiding the negative outcomes as much as possible. In this handbook, I give you a brief explanation of some of the various factors that may affect your health and well-being while flying and ways for you to arrive at your destination feeling happy and healthy.

There are many tips here. My philosophy is for you to take what you want and leave the rest. Even if you don't seem affected by taking long flights, there is still something here for you. I encourage you to adopt healthy habits that minimize the effects of the stress of air travel so that you can be a happy healthy jetsetter, too!

# 1

# CHALLENGES FACING THE JETSETTER

"Most travelers unknowingly assume far greater risks. Flight crews and frequent flyers are susceptible to a host of health problems, from cancer and cardiovascular disease, to vision and healing loss, to mental disorders and cognitive decline. Short-term problems from jet lag include the obvious fatigue and loss of concentration but also irritability and loss of appetite," says Life Science.[23]

## STRESS

Flying will be stressful. Even if it is the starting point of a pleasurable vacation, stress is one of the inevitable major strains on a traveler. I would love to help you avoid losing your pleasure and productivity due to the consequences of flying.

The effects of the stressors of air travel can make you more vulnerable to becoming ill after flying. Some stressors of air travel include:

Crowds, lines, rude people, flight delays, reschedules, and inconvenient sudden changes

Exposure to radiation (Solar, Cosmic, Nuclear and Wi-Fi and EMF)

Changing cabin pressure, lack of oxygen, ozone toxicity, cabin air pollution and toxic chemicals

Dehydration

Immobility

Time zone disruption

Exposure to MRSA, E. coli, bacterial, viral, and parasitic infections

Unrest/anxiety/insomnia/diarrhea/constipation

An assault of sound and vibration from proximity to jet engines/ sound pollution

Getting to the airport (traffic, time concerns, parking), getting checked in, navigating security, finding a seat, and even the boarding process require you to be on your toes. As if just getting through the airport and onto the plane isn't enough, the stress continues once you're in your seat. More stressors confront you on the plane, including radiation, dehydration, ozone poisoning, pressure changes, rude or sick neighbors and problems with comfort and sleep. The rhythmic working of your organs and glands can get thrown off and your metabolism slows. We're all familiar with jet lag!

## RADIATION

Radiation exposure is damaging to your DNA. The effects of damaged DNA can manifest in innumerable ways. Radiation accumulates in the body, so the effects can take time to manifest. Cancer is a condition resulting from DNA mutation. There are other results not as well documented, but still damaging to your body.

In fact, aircrews have been classified as radiation workers. Most people are not aware that the jet stream is where radioactive pollution from nuclear accidents and detonations is circulating. When flying west to east, the jet is most certainly using the jet stream to save fuel. Even though you can't see it, smell it, or taste it and you probably don't read about it, radiation is one of the most concerning exposures you'll experience in the air.

In *The Invisible Passenger: Radiation Risks*, a book by Robert J. Barish, PhD, he enumerates some of the facts of cosmic or solar radiation while flying:

- Your solar radiation exposure doubles with every 6,500 feet of altitude.

- Solar flares can increase your radiation exposure 10 to 20 times.

- Pilot cancer rates for four major cancers are high; in some cases much higher than average.

- Pregnant women should be particularly concerned about radiation levels on airplanes.

- Radiation levels in a jetliner are occasionally so high that in a nuclear power plant these levels would require warning employees not to spend any more time in the area than necessary to do their jobs. As a matter of fact, the FAA has classified flight crews as radiation workers ever since 1994.

In Europe, all EU air carriers are required to provide training to their crews in radiation and dose assessment.

These facts do not take into consideration the radiation released from nuclear weapon detonations and nuclear accidents, like Fukushima. The radioisotopes rise up from Chernobyl, Fukushima, and other nuclear disasters or detonations and then circulate in the jet stream. When flying in the jet stream, which is where most planes fly for the longest duration from one city to another, radiation is high.

Wi-Fi is the type of radiation that damages the Van Der Waal's bonds of the DNA, whereas the ionizing radioactivity discussed above does more damage to the DNA by disorganizing the DNA's covalent bonds. On an airplane Wi-Fi signals are being transmitted and received inside of a metal container, i.e., the fuselage. Hence, the Wi-Fi microwave bandwidth signal exposure is increased exponentially because it continues to bounce around inside the fuselage, passing over you over and over and over again until each Wi-Fi signal fades out.

## IMMOBILITY

Another possible complication of air travel is *traveler's thrombosis*. This can cause blood clots to form in your body while you are sitting inactive at high altitudes. These clots usually form in your legs and then can travel to your lungs, heart or brain, where they can lead to death. A study in *The Lancet* found that 1 percent of travelers developed a clot.[1] With about 2 billion air travelers annually, that extrapolates to 20 million deep vein thrombosis (DVT) cases, leading potentially to thousands of deaths.

Immobility, low oxygen levels, low humidity and cabin pressure can slow your metabolism, and cause extreme dehydration, which means all body processes are slowed down including your metabolism, circulation and digestion. This is part of the reason for recommending that you hydrate well and avoid eating just before or on board the flight. These conditions can also lead to constipation. Symptoms of constipation can be headache, feeling bloated and generally uncomfortable.

## TOXINS AND PATHOGENS

In flight, you will certainly be exposed to environmental toxins and pathogens. After flying, you have an increased risk of catching a cold—over 100 times higher than if you had not flown, according to a study in the *Journal of Environmental Health Research*.[2] It's more than the people sneezing next to you. There are a variety of jetsetting pathogenic bacteria found everywhere. In the seat back pocket, MRSA can live up to five days! E. Coli bacteria are found not just in the lavatory, but also on almost every surface inside the plane and in most of the onboard water. This means the tap water and hand washing water in the lavatory are most likely contaminated with E.Coli.

Introduced in 1999, Aerotoxic Syndrome is a little-known term given to long and short-term symptoms caused by exposure to cabin air in jet aircraft that is contaminated with toxic chemicals.[21] The Aerotoxic Association said, "if you become suddenly violently ill on a plane – or if you have symptoms after deplaning, such as headaches, flu-like symptoms or disorientation – it may not be old-fashioned, run-of-the-mill airsickness or jet lag. If you have noticed symptoms of chronic fatigue, depression or a nervous disorder similar to Parkinson's disease occurring soon after a flight, you could be a victim of Aerotoxic Syndrome".[21]

One of the likely chemicals you are exposed to are fire retardants. Much research is available about the deleterious affects of exposure to fire retardants in flight attendants. This footnote will learn you to research from the BioMed Central called "Exposure to Flame Retardant Chemicals on Commercial Airplanes."[36] If you search the internet, you'll find a large body of information on the chemical toxins you might be exposed to during your flight.

I'm not wanting to launch into a disclosure of all the toxins you may be exposed to, as much as let you know how to protect yourself.

The longer the flight is, the more potential for your health to be challenged. Many of the toxic effects of flying are cumulative, like exposure to radiation and chemical toxins such as jet fuel fumes.

# 2

# FOOD AND DRINK

**The World Health Organization, in their 2017 statement on Travel and Health,**[3] **say: "Although some of the events that cause stress cannot be predicted, taking precautions may reduce travel-related stress."**

All food and drink on the aircraft are to be scrutinized for their benefit-to-cost ratio in terms of your well-being. Generally, you will want to drink more and eat less. Staying well hydrated is helpful for mitigating all the effects of stress you'll encounter. A well hydrated body functions better than a dehydrated one.

## HYDRATION

Staying hydrated will save you suffering, time, and money. It might even save you from missing part of your trip because you got sick. Dehydration will occur during air travel, unless you consciously hydrate to compensate for the fluid loss during your flight.

Do you know that water makes up more than half the weight of your body? Dehydration happens when you taken in less than enough water. Then, your body can not function optimally or look its best.

Every part of your body –every cell, tissue, and organ- is dependent on water to work the way it should.

Water is needed to maintain your body temperature, keep you joints lubricated and to remove waste.

The effects of being dehydrated show on your face and skin, as well as affect your mood, your energy, your immunity and overall well-being. Staying hydrated is essential to your health. It is important for keeping your heartbeat regular as well as keeping your blood well-oxygenated. In fact, staying hydrated is vitally important for all bodily functions.

While bodies are most comfortable at around 50% humidity, an airplane's cabin humidity is less than 20% and can go as low as 4%. This is like being in a desert! Pathogens can get into your body through parched skin, nose, mouth, and throat membranes. A three-hour flight can dry out 1.5 liters of water from your body![33] If you fall asleep, and mouth breath, you lose even more precious body water.

Lets take a look at the symptoms of dehydration. Fatigue is often the first sign of dehydration. Dehydration may cause you to be dizzy, or confused and constipated. Headaches, light-headedness, brain fog, rapid heartbeat, strong hunger, dry mouth, muscle cramps, and constipation are possible symptoms of dehydration. If you experience any of these, drink more water and see if it helps.

If you urinate less than every two hours, and/or the urine is dark colored and/or only a small amount; these can be signs of dehydration. Well-hydrated adults will urinate every two hours during the day.

Urine is clear or only lightly yellow, unless you taking something that colors your urine yellow, like B vitamins.

By the time you feel thirsty, it is likely you are already dehydrated! Having a dry mouth may be one of the last signs of dehydration. Feeling hungry can be a sign you are dehydrated. I suggest that you hydrate and see if the hunger goes away.

The symptoms of dehydration are different for young children and adults.[3] Infants or young children may have no wet diapers for three hours; they might have no tears when crying, dry mouth and tongue, be listless or irritable, and the soft spot on the top of the skull may sink in. When you fly with an infant, attempt to have them nurse or take a bottle during landing and take off. This may help adjust the pressure in their sinuses and ears, and prevent pain for them, as well as provide hydration.

**The best tip that helps you mitigate all stressors is to stay hydrated.** This means staying hydrated every day. It is not about just loading up on water while you are flying.

Many people think that if they are swallowing a liquid it is hydrating for their body. This is not true. Some beverages are actually dehydrating and in addition are acidifying and filled with sugar and chemicals, such as: alcohol, coffee, soda and many bottled fruit juices or sweet teas. These are best avoided.

## SUGGESTIONS

- You want be very well hydrated when you begin your trip and stay hydrated throughout your trip. Have you ever taken a selfie before you left, and another when you landed? The effects of dehydration will be visible on your face!

- The morning of flying, drink 16 ounces of water as quickly as possible. (I add 1/8 teaspoon salt to 16 ounces water. See supplement section for details.) Drinking 16 ounces of water quickly, will not only hydrate you, but may also facilitate your bowel movement.

- It is easy to get constipated during travel. Wake up early enough so you can eliminate before you leave for the airport, if possible.

- Then continue to drink water, sipping. Fill up with as much water as you can before going through security.

- Ask at the Airport Information Counter if they have a fountain of filtered water inside the terminal, or call to ask in advance.

- You may want to look online or ask at the Information Counter at the airport if there is a juice bar, smoothie stand, or a café where fresh vegetable or fruit salads are available. These probably have a preservative on them, but this is an option if you need to eat something water-rich.

I've found organic juice in a few terminals. Drinking fresh organic vegetable juices are helpful for hydration. (If you are in a third world country, then you should avoid raw food, juice and smoothies unless you are certain of the cleanliness of the water and produce.)

- I carry a water filter. I use the filter for *all* the water. I use it for tap water and bottled water. If you don't have a filter and can't find acceptable bottled water, I've found that Starbucks uses filtered water in most locations.

- Even if you have to drink unfiltered tap water or bottled water from the terminal, it is better to drink it and be hydrated than to be dehydrated, in my opinion.


**Onboard**

Since 911, the airlines only allow you to bring your carry on liquids in 3.4 ounce (100ml) size or less (by volume) containers, in a 1 quart-sized, clear, plastic, zip-top bag; 1 bag per passenger placed in screening bin at security check points[30]. If you want to, you can fill about 8, 3 ounce bottles with water to which you will add your salt, and/or supplements. Then you'll have about 24 ounces of nutrified water that you can drink onboard.

**I've found that the more I can drink just before I fly, the less I need while onboard to stay hydrated.**

- Do not rely on the airline to have enough bottled water onboard. You may want to purchase water in the terminal. A couple brands that are usually available in the terminal that have better reputations are Smartwater™ and Fiji™. (It is better to drink water and refill your bottles from the fountain in the terminal than to be dehydrated.)

- Drink 8 ounces of water for every hour you are on the plane at a minimum.

- Before you land is a good time to load up on water. Drink all the water you have brought on board so that you can go to the restroom in the airport terminal rather than on the plane.

- Do not drink the onboard tap water without using your filter. Most likely the water in the tea or coffee on board is tainted with E. coli.

- The canned tomato juice might be the best choice on board, if you are out of water and without a filter.

- Although eating before or during a flight is not optimal, if you have no water, you could eat fresh organic juicy fruits or vegetables as an alternative hydration method. I like to bring along a fruit or vegetable salad in a baggie. Fresh fruits—such as juicy oranges, apples, pears, and grapefruit—and/ or vegetables, such as celery or carrot sticks, jicama, even salsa or guacamole and all vegetable sprouts travel well in a baggie. They are light and hydrating but also satisfy your hunger. (If you use the tray table, be sure to sanitize it, and use a napkin as a tablecloth. Tray tables are notorious for harboring bad bacteria.)

- Chronic Dehydration: Some people are chronically dehydrated. If you have trouble staying hydrated, try putting a pinch of high quality salt into each glass of water. This should help you rehydrate.

The average person needs anywhere from 1 tsp to 2 tablespoons of salt per day to keep the sodium potassium pump functioning properly. (You may get some of this salt from food, like celery or seaweed.) The sodium potassium pump cannot reach enough head pressure to inject the fresh water inside the cell to rehydrate the cell without enough salt. This is one reason that some people drink a lot of water but do not seem to be getting hydrated.

Supplements like Scalar Salts™, Crystal Energy Tincture™, Mega-Hydrate™, Willard Water™, and other preparations make the water more absorbable. I have sources on KatharineClarkRN.com for some of these items.

- Since your body (metabolism) systems slows down while in the air, you can end up with bad breath, particularly if you fall asleep. A small bottle of mint breath freshener can be quite refreshing and helpful. I don't recommend chewing gum, or sweet mints. You can find a lovely honey mint breath freshener that has no artificial ingredients in the health food store, its made with edible essential oil.

- Chronic Constipation: If you have a tendency to constipation, you'll be more likely to suffer after a flight because of the dehydration and immobility. Constipation and bloating can lead to a headache, fatigue, and irritability. I list a couple of constipation remedies in the supplement section that you may want to use for prevention if you know you are inclined to constipation. You may want to take a stool softener and/or a laxative the night before you fly, the morning of your flight, and the night afterwards.

Adding the high quality salt will also help move your bowels. The peristaltic action of the colon is an electrical function and requires electrolytes/ minerals. Add these to your water with a high quality salt. 1/8 tsp of this salt with 16 oz of water may also facilitate this electrically induced peristalsis.

*My mother always told me, "Where there is a will, there is a way." In 2002, I was flying out of Manila. The airline had a scale set up at the gate to weigh carry-on luggage, limited to 25 pounds. With my water inside, my bag was over the allowable weight. I used my belt to strap the water bottles around my waist, and carried about four liters of water onto the plane as body weight!*

## The What and When of Liquids

Here are some general insights to drinking liquid.

- **How Much:** We're commonly told to drink eight 8-ounce glasses of water a day (64 ounces, or almost 2 liters) to keep hydrated. Another guide to hydration is to drink half an ounce of water for every pound of body weight, so a 100-pound person would drink 50 ounces a day to break even. You may be getting some hydration from juicy fruits and fresh vegetables in your diet which may cut back on the water you need to drink. If you're sweating from heat or exercise you'll need to drink more water.

  For added stresses of air travel, consider ¾ to full body weight in ounces with the appropriate amount of salt to truly hydrate the body during flights. All kinds of factors influence your hydration, but this is a good standard. I'll talk about other ways to identify poor hydration later.

- **Beverage Temperature:** Consider drinking liquids at room temperature. Your body has to expend energy to regulate your core body temperature. Drinking ice water is stressful to your system. When drinks are at room temperature, they are closer to body temperature and your body has to use less energy to regulate your core temperature, and you have more energy for feeling good! Extremes of hot or cold drinks may harm your teeth, too. If you love ice-cold drinks, see if you can wean yourself away from them. A hot organic herbal tea you can take to the airport in the morning is a great way to relax and hydrate. Very hot and icy drinks can also harm your teeth.

- **When to Drink:** During meals: I say, drink up to 30 minutes before a meal and not for an hour or two after. Drinking too much liquid with your meals can dilute the digestive enzymes needed to digest your food. Have only around a half-cup with your meal. Chew your food well to mix it with saliva in your mouth, which contain the digestive enzymes for starch digestion.

  What you drink with your meal affects your digestion. If you drink more than ½ cup during a meal, you run the risk of diluting your digestive power. If you drink something that is sweet and/or acidic, like soda, alcohol, coffee or black tea, you add to the complexity of digestion and your body needs more energy to digest it.

- **What Not To Drink:** Caffeine is a diuretic. Coffee, alcohol, black tea, green tea, some sodas, energy drinks and some juices have caffeine naturally or caffeine added. Ideally, you drink these in moderation, if at all, on the day before and the day of a flight. Drinking sweet and/or acidic beverages requires your body to use minerals to help maintain your acid/alkaline balance. Adding salt to your water will help you replenish some of these minerals. Over time, coffee, soda, alcohol, black tea, or liquids with sugar and other sweeteners may contribute to chronic dehydration.

I hope that by the time you read this that clean water and organic food choices are widely available in every airport and on every flight!

**Onboard water**

- **The water, ice, coffee, tea, and even opened bottled water served on board may be contaminated with E. coli.** If you do drink airline beverages, be sure they are canned or from a sealed bottle. It may be that canned tomato juice is your best on-board choice to provide some hydration. If you need to hydrate and no fresh fruit, veggies or water is available, then make the best choice you can from what is available.

- **Carry a small portable water filter.** There are small portable water filters that you can carry on board which exceed the National Science Foundation standards for removal of giardia, bacteria, viruses, cryptosporidium, chlorine, fluoride, heavy metals, waterborne chemicals, and some radioactive substances. (Filters will not remove the radioisotope of hydrogen known as tritium because it is too small. That is another reason I use Rad Zero™ periodically. Follow the manufacture's directions for Rad Zero™ on FreshAndAlive.com)

**Nutrify your water.** What you can add to water to make it more palatable and/or absorbable:

- Add a pinch of high quality salt up to ½ tsp in 16 oz of water.

- I like to pack a bottle or baggie with something to supplement the beverages; I carry packets of Oxylent™, a delicious multivitamin mineral powder you add to your water. Gaia Herbs is another good source for powers that make water more palatable and nutritious.

- Read labels! Don't buy sugar, artificial sweeteners, colors or flavors. Even "natural flavors" can include MSG, so they are best avoided.

- I like Essentials™ or Essentials Blend™ Essentials come in packets, which are easier to travel with. You can open the capsules into the water or simply swallow them. (LivingLightFood.com)

- You can bring miso soup in single-serving packets. Mix the packet into hot or cold water to make a tasty, remineralizing, fortifying beverage.

- If you are hooked on sweet flavors, you can make water tasty and sweet by adding stevia. Stevia comes flavored—lemon, cinnamon, or butterscotch. Be sure to use only a little. Stevia's bad reputation for an unpleasant taste comes when you use too much. Add a little, you can add more if needed.

- Using herbal tea: You can bring organic herbal tea bags and add them to room temperature pure water in a bottle. They will still steep into the water and give it flavor and color. Traditional Medicinals have a whole line of organic tea bags. You can choose the one to pick you up, relax you, make you go, or fortify your immunity. Bring a small selection! If you like it sweet, try using stevia rather than sugar or honey to sweeten your drink.

My favorite tea to take is Hibiscus tea because of the vitamin C it contains. Chamomile is calming. It can be fun to choose tasty teas with extra benefits.

I often buy powdered Hibiscus Flowers, Rose Hips, Camu Camu Berries and Stevia from Mountain Rose Herbs. Then I mix them, and put a little bit in a carry on bottle. I can add the powder to water and make a tasty, pink colored, vitamin C drink!


**About Alcohol**

Beer, wine, and liquor are acidifying and dehydrating. In the air your blood alcohol levels rise higher at higher altitudes than at sea level.

Drinking alcohol slows down your metabolism, reduces blood oxygenation, lowers your immunity, and kills brain cells. Alcohol is going to challenge your digestion, your immune system, your mood, your rest, and your overall well-being, especially before or during a flight.

* Save alcohol for a celebration on the ground, or avoid it all together.

## Remember:

If your immune system is strong and you are well hydrated, you may be exposed to pathogens without being adversely affected. Pathogens are everywhere. Whether or not you get sick depends on your immunity.

## Taking Care of Your Skin

Maintaining your skin integrity is vital! Your skin integrity is one of your main defenses against pathogens. When your skin or the membranes of your nose, mouth and eyes are dry and cracked, they cannot provide a barrier against pathogens.

* Staying hydrated will help keep your eyes, nose, and throat moist and intact. There are jetsetting bugs from around the world in the airport and on the plane! I can't emphasize how important it is to stay hydrated all the time. Intact mucus membranes form a barrier to pathogens. Cracked ones do not.

- Apply a good moisturizing lotion all over your skin. after your shower, before your flight. What you apply to your skin will go in! Unless it is a long flight, a spritzer will be adequate for refreshing your face. I love rose water. Remember to keep it in a container that is less than 3 ounces!

- If you're on a long haul, or you need moisture onboard, you want something that you do not put your fingers into and possibly contaminate the whole jar. I'm recommending a stick of cacao butter or a tube of moisturizer. If you have oily skin, you might want to use an aloe-based moisturizer. Remember to use clean hands!

- When you want to moisturize your lips and nostrils, raw virgin coconut, sesame, or avocado oil, cocoa butter, or shea butter would work. Again, you're going to eat this, or get food grade, organic lip moisturizers.

- If you are dehydrated or inclined to dry eyes, then bring drops. I have used Sovereign Silver Spray in my eyes.

- You can bring an aloe-based nasal lubricant or use XClear™, which is excellent and comes in a small travel size. You can also use coconut oil to coat the nostrils. There are a few products for your eyes and nose that are homeopathic. Just find something natural and non-toxic, not filled with chemicals.

Products you put onto your body are absorbed through your skin into your body, so be selective about what you put on your skin, in your mouth, eyes and nose. Just find something that is organic and edible to put on and in your body!

## FOOD

Did you know that a third of your taste buds get numbed out when flying at high altitudes? The dryness and changes in air pressure may affect your ears, sinuses, and taste. In addition, your metabolism is slowed during air travel.

The best research says that not eating during a flight is a very effective way to minimize jet lag.[4] Thirst is often experienced as hunger, so drink more rather than eating unless you have a medical consideration that dictates that you eat.

Because your digestive system is slowed while flying at high altitude, it is best to avoid eating. If you become hungry, see if you can satisfy yourself with healthy liquids and super foods just before and during your flight.

I use Super Foods and Nutritious Drink Enhancers listed in the Supplement Section. Super Foods travel well and are great sources of easy to digest and assimilate nutrition. Having super foods can help satisfy your hunger.

## SUGGESTIONS

- Postpone eating from an hour before the flight until you land, if possible. Drinking may subdue your hunger. If you must eat, bring or buy juicy fruit or veggies.

- Postponing a meal until you land is also a simple way to help synchronize your internal body clock.[5] The idea is to plan your big meal around the local dining time of your destination, which is a great way to get adjusted to a time zone even before you arrive.

- When you arrive, if you're hungry eat a good light meal. Get to sleep at around 10 p.m. local time at your destination.

  Avoid overeating, and see if you can choose a simple meal such as soup, oatmeal, salad or fruit. (When in 3rd world countries you may want to stick with cooked food, unless you are sure of the source of water and produce.)

- Be sure to take some digestive enzymes and probiotics at bedtime.

- Using a sleep aid can help you adjust your body clock. There are gentle homeopathic sleep aids, and Gaia Herbs has a few wonderful herbal formulas.

- You might also want to use a little laxative to keep yourself regular and counter the dehydration of the flight and the new time zone.

- Avoid alcohol, as it is both dehydrating and debilitating and can add to jet lag.

- Choose the healthiest food. It is smart to limit sweets because they are acidifying and can affect your blood sugar balance. Having your blood sugar go up and down can make your mood go up and down. This isn't something you need while you are traveling.

**If you must eat on board**

If you are too hungry to wait, or the flight is very long: simply snack lightly and mindfully. Chew more, and take time to eat. Don't rush it!

- Choose the healthiest food you can find or bring. Bring or buy juice fruits or vegetables.

- Bring your own snacks to nibble on, like fresh fruit or vegetable salad in a baggie, or sprouted dried nuts and seeds with berries. Many whole foods are prohibited on flights to Hawaii and international destinations. However, if the fruit or vegetable is peeled, deseeded, and prepared into a salad, you can take it on board to enjoy later.

- Pick foods that are colorful. Rich deeply pigmented foods are more nutritious and known for antioxidants. Dark green vegetables have chlorophyll, which helps your blood carry more oxygen as well as being known for being nutrient dense. Choose sweet potatoes over white potatoes, for example.

- I like to keep a pack of organic nori seaweed sheets in my travel bag. Nori is the thin black seaweed that is wrapped around the rice in sushi at the Japanese restaurant. It is rich in minerals and antioxidants and has sodium alginate, which provides protection against radiation damage. I eat the nori as is, or use it with fresh vegetables, salads, and soups, or stuff the nori sheets with guacamole at a Mexican place in the terminal during my layover. I have been known to make nori rolls at home with sprouts, tomatoes, garlic, and avocado and put them in a baggie to eat on a long flight or after the flight is over.

- Dehydrated crackers, snack mixes, dried fruits and nuts travel well, but you need to hydrate even more when eating dried foods. If possible, eat them with something moist, like leaves of cabbage, carrot and celery sticks, sprouts or an apple.

- If you're empty handed, it is better to grab a fruit or veggie salad in the terminal, rather than risk having to eat processed, prepackaged snacks available on board. Check the Environmental Working Group website (www.ewg.org) for the "Clean 15 and the Dirty Dozen." Each year EWG updates this list with the fruits and vegetables that are safe to eat non-organic, and the ones that you want to have as organic. Usually avocados are on the Clean 15 list. (If you are in a 3rd world country you may want to eat only cooked food and avoid produce unless you are certain of its cleanliness.)

- Sprouts are a great choice. It is easy to have *sprouts* available to eat even when you're on the road. Lentils, fenugreek, mung, adzuki, and sunflower all are road-worthy sprouts. Pack them inside a baggie. You'll be eating living food; food that is alive when you eat it. Sprouts are water-rich, nutrient dense and easy to digest.


- **Airplane Food:** Meals on domestic flights are rare. Most flights over 2 hours have snacks for sale that are full of processed foods.

  I think its better to bring your own food, or grab something in the terminal rather than take your chances with on board service.


Back in the day: I was served a meat appetizer with my vegetarian meal in first class on two different occasions. I'm pretty easygoing, but I did let the airline's customer service know about it. As you might guess, I routinely bring my own food and never take a tray in flight.


## Grow Your Own Travel Garden!

I sprouted and ate raw food all the way through Nepal, India, and Thailand in the early 1980s. I purchased a plastic bucket to use as my "kitchen." I purified water with my filter and iodine, then rinsed the sprouts in the purified water and soaked the seeds in it. I then used the purified water to scrub vegetables before I grated and ate them. To transport my mini-garden, I put my sprout bags (with the sprouts growing inside) into my bucket and covered the top with a clean towel. When I crossed a border, I discarded my bucket and started with a new one in the new country. This system worked very well for me. In foreign countries, hand washing also becomes very important. Be sure to carry your own clean soap and towel. Using a soiled towel will soil your hands. I also carry soap nuts so that I can wash my own clothes and towel in my sprouting bucket! Shecology.com soap nuts are antibacterial, anti-fungal, and antiviral and can be used for dishes or laundry. (Free Sprouting Guide on KatharineClarkRN.com)


**SUPPLEMENTS** (Sources listed in Supplements Section)

I personally use Digestive Enzymes, Probiotics and super foods every day. I'll share what works for me.

- Digestive Enzymes: Taking plant-based digestive enzymes is a smart practice anytime. Supplementing your body with plant-based digestive enzymes helps your body in a number of ways.

  However when eating just before or during a flight, be sure to swallow a capsule or two. Taking enzymes can prevent the consequences of a variety of indiscretions such as eating poor quality food, over eating, or eating in flight.

These enzymes will help your bodily functions overall and are safe for anyone except people with gastric ulcers, gastric hyper mobility like Crohns, or Colitis. If you have a gastric dysfunction, check with your doctor before taking digestive enzymes.

- Probiotics: Although I will discuss them later, travelers who understand their body will want to boost their friendly flora by taking probiotics along for the ride. A 5-6 hour flight really stresses your gut flora, (healthy bacteria). Supplement with a good probiotic after every flight and make it a point to eat some good yogurt, sauerkraut, or kimchi unless you have a condition where probiotic foods or supplements are contraindicated.

# 3

## TOXINS AND PATHOGENS

**Airplanes are full of bacteria, viruses, and chemical hazards.** A two-year study, funded by the Federal Aviation Administration's Airliner Cabin Environmental Research Center,[6] revealed that disease-causing bacteria could survive for up to a week on surfaces inside plane cabins. Staphylococcus aureus and MRSA (Methicillin-resistant Staphylococcus aureus), bacterium that could cause infections, skin disease, pneumonia and sepsis, lived the longest (168 hours); Escherichia coli (E. coli), which can cause urinary tract infection, respiratory illness, diarrhea, and death, was found to survive outside a body and on surfaces for 96 hours outside a body. E. Coli has been found on the seats and in the water supply, not just in the lavatory! MRSA has been found in seat-back pockets and on tray tables. Beware of the contents of the seat back pocket. The magazine is never cleaned and often handled.

**You are 20-110 times more likely to catch a cold after flying.**[34] The dry air in the plane's cabin affects your mucus membranes, which are the front line of defense for the immune system. You are assaulted by an array of international pathogens, and you are deprived to clean well-oxygenated air, while being irradiated at higher than normal levels. All these stress your immune system. Be sure to stay well hydrated.

The dirtiest places[7] on a plane are:

- Plastic tray tables—win the top spot as the dirtiest surface of all. If you must use the table, sanitize it with wipes and still use a napkin as a cover. Make sure not to eat food directly off the surface of the table.

- Lavatory flush button—while the bathrooms themselves are actually fairly clean since these are sanitized more often, the flush button itself is nasty. Remember to open the restroom door with a paper towel on the way out and shut the door before the flush happens.

- Seat back pocket—may have been stuffed with trash, dirty tissues, used diapers, and more. Some planes with quick turnarounds may not be able to empty out the pockets, and certainly not enough time to disinfect them.

  Don't use the seat back pocket or the magazine inside.

- Aisle seats—you thought they were the best seats and I think they are too, but the corner of the top of the seat harbors germs from everyone who walks by and holds on for support, especially on the way back from the restroom.

  New research shows that the window seat passenger is less likely to catch a cold. I still prefer the aisle because there is less radiation there and it is much easier to get up and move around.

- Seatbelt buckle—another dirty place! Use a tissue to touch it or sanitize your hands after touching it. It is against your clothes so another reason to launder your clothes soon after the flight.

- Overhead air vent

## SUGGESTIONS

A strong immune system is your best defense. Staying hydrated is essential to your immunity!

- Avoid touching your face, eyes, mouth, nose, and ears with your hands unless you clean them first or use a tissue. Your hands are probably loaded with pathogens, so keep them away from your mucus membranes (eyes, nose, mouth, genitals).

- Use tissues as needed to touch surfaces, especially in the bathroom.

- If you are so inclined: bring non-toxic sanitizer or wipes to clean all areas of your seat, seat back, armrests and tray tables. If you are in the aisle row, clean the edge of your seat, where passers by touch.

- I love to use Young Living "Thieves™" spray and wipes. They are effective, non-toxic, and smell great. For hand sanitizer, I use Neutralizer Gel™ or spray.

- Airplane lavatories are particularly "dirty". Dress appropriately. You don't want the hem of your pants, dress, or skirt touching the floor or the toilet. In the airport restroom, use a paper towel or tissue to touch anything and every thing. You even want to wear plastic gloves!

I think this might be excessive and wasteful but one person I know carries an inexpensive raincoat, which he wears over his clothes before the flight. After the flight he discards it and washes his hands.

- In the terminal: use your carry-on to hold your purse and/or briefcase rather than setting them on the floor.

- Once you're off the plane, wash yourself and your clothes as soon as possible. Use soap and warm/hot water. If you have slippers that you used on the plane to go to the lavatory, wash these as well and put them into a clean baggie for the next flight. Most infectious organisms can live outside the body for days; hanging out on your clothes or body.[28] Another reason to shower and to wash your clothes is to remove radiation that can also linger on your skin and clothes.

Automated flush toilets and sink water, and paper towel dispensers are very helpful for keeping your hands clean and many airports now have them.

**SUPPLEMENTS** (Sources listed in the Sources section.)

- I use supplements to support my immune system, which are listed, at the end of the book. These include Digestive Enzymes, Probiotics, Super Food Wild Essentials, Enhanced Alive Iodine™, RadNeutral™, SuperOxygenated Water™ and vitamin C.

- Use high quality probiotics that are made by a reputable company. It is estimated that around 90% of the cells in your body are actually bacteria. These friendly probiotics are the basis of your immune system. Drinking alcohol, coffee, tap water, many medications, stress and flying at high altitude all compromise your gut bacteria. Therefore, replacing friendly flora regularly is a smart way to be sure you are full of the friendly bugs (friendly flora) called probiotics, rather than being host to the bad bugs. I use Spectrabiotic™ before during and after every flight. You can find high-quality probiotics in a health food store. Use your air purifier, and/or a particle mask with charcoal for airborne toxins and pathogens

## Airborne Pathogens & Poor Air Quality

I hate smelling the airplane fuel exhaust that inevitably enters the cabin before you take off. The Aerotoxic Association has estimated that almost 200,000 passengers are exposed to and negatively affected by toxic chemicals in the cabin. The most common symptoms include: fatigue, blurred vision, burning eyes, shaking, dizziness, disorientation, loss of balance, memory loss, tinnitus, tingling fingers, but can also include seizures, respiratory distress, vomiting, severe headaches, neurological damage, brain inflammation, heart spasms, and even sudden cardiac arrest from inflammation of the heart muscle caused by neurotoxins.[23]

Air quality during flight is compromised in a variety of ways. The air in the cabin is drawn in through the engine compartments and then recirculates. Cabin air is likely to be contaminated with neurotoxic chemicals from the engine compartments and jet fuel exhaust. There are innumerable airborne viruses, bacteria, even parasites that are in circulation. Your body also has to compensate for low oxygen, low humidity and ozone toxicity.

The interior of the plane is routinely sprayed with fire retardant.


**SUGGESTIONS**

* Once again, stay hydrated!

* I always wear a personal air purifier. Small personal air filters clean the air in a small circle around the unit. Wear one around your neck, inside your shirt, to propel fresher air into your breathing zone. It will protect your companion as well. These air purifiers emit a constant stream of healthy negative ions that force airborne pollutants away from your personal space, giving

you a three-foot sphere of cleaner, healthier air around your head. It cleans the air of pollutants (viruses, pollen, smoke, molds, and dust mites) that traditional air purifiers leave behind.

I love. FilterStream AirTamer personal air purifiers clean your air by removing airborne pollutants (e.g. viruses, bacteria, pollen, dust, etc.) from your personal space!     I have a link for AirTamer on KatharineClarkRN.com.

- For protection against airborne bacteria, viruses and toxins, I use an Air Purifying Particle Face Mask with activated carbon filter rated N99. I like the Organic ones from VogMask.com. They offer protection against gases, smells, all (Particulate Matter) PM; PM2.5, PM0.3, pollen, smoke and pathogens such as viruses and bacteria.

If wearing a mask is not for you, try the Nose Filters.   They are almost invisible and remove a great deal of pollution including fumes from the air. Charcoal cellulose ones come in various sizes and some have replaceable filters. I have these on KatharineClarkRN.com as well.

- You could also buy Thieves Oil from Young Living, Doterra has On Guard, or do an online search or ask at your health food store for a similar essential oil spray to purify your self, your seat area, surfaces, and especially the lavatory.   Just remember to get a small size that you can carry on the plane. Thieves Essential oil is an ancient recipe known for purification; it's anti-bacterial, anti-fungal, and anti-viral, and comes under a few brand names.

## SUPPLEMENTS

* There are varieties of food-based supplements that are used to strengthen immunity.

  I always load up on Enhanced Alive Iodine™. Enhanced Alive Iodine™ is antiseptic and also loads your thyroid so it won't need to uptake radioactive iodine.    (Follow manufacture's instructions. See source in my supplement section)

  I have others listed in the Supplements Section

# 4

## OTHER POTENTIAL PROBLEMS

### DEEP VEIN THROMBOSIS

**Statistics say you are 40% more likely to experience deep vein thrombosis (DVT)[8] [9] after a flight then if you did not fly at all.** DVT is such a serious threat to your health that airline magazines have a section in the back about exercises to do while in flight. I'm going to tell you what they say, and make a few more suggestions.

Researchers from the University of Illinois at Chicago[10] recently found that you can make sitting healthier than standing by moving your legs more while you sit. Craig Horswill, the study's lead author, said those sitting at a desk while periodically moving their feet fared better than those sitting or standing still.

**SUGGESTIONS:**

Basically, you want to keep your circulation going by moving.

**In the terminal:**

* Resist the urge to take that moving walkway; use your legs to get extra blood flowing before you board and after you fly. Walking moves all your muscles, blood, and lymph. Lymph carries toxins

so they can be eliminated. Walk whenever you can: pace while you're waiting for your flight to board, or walk around the terminal. Take the stairs in the airport. You need the exercise to help oxygenate your body, as well as for the elimination of toxins. You can reduce that tired feeling by walking around and staying hydrated.

**Onboard:**

- While in your seat keep your circulation going: repeatedly tighten & release your legs and buttocks, and flex your legs as much as possible. I like to do little leg lifts with my tummy tight. Might as well get in a little abdominal workout! Frequently rotate and flex your ankles. Point your toes, flex your feet, and wiggle your toes.

- Get up and walk around a few times, breathing deeply. You can even do some squats, jump or jog in place near the galley! Once you get to your destination, take a shower and put on fresh clothes, drink some water, and take a walk!

- Wear loose-fitting clothes! You don't want to obstruct blood flow with constricting clothes, belts, shoes, or socks. You know your feet swell on a plane because your shoes feel tight by the end of the flight.

- If you are vulnerable to DVT or fly often, you might want to wear compression stockings. Compression stockings prevent the venous blood from pooling and help it return to the heart.

Compression Socks come in different sizes and compression levels. Get help from a knowledgeable professional: a physical therapist, a podiatrist or physician, in picking the right size and style for you. Search online for a good pair with cotton, bamboo or silk content, since natural fibers help your skin breathe. Bamboo is naturally antimicrobial. Be sure your socks do not contain "microban" which has been shown to be toxic.[35]

Clots can appear up to 30 days after a flight. If after the flight you experience pain or swelling in your leg, or difficulty walking because of pain in your legs, you need to be checked for a clot.

- Research has shown that Pycnogenol Reduces the Risk of Deep Vein Clots (Thrombosis): A 2004 study[20] found that Pycnogenol (dosage: 100 mg, two capsules between 2 and 3 hours before flights; two capsules taken 6 hours after the flight, and one capsule the next day) administered to subjects on flights averaging 8 hours and 15 minutes, in length resulted in zero deep vein thrombosis events, and only non-thrombotic, localized phlebitis (inflammation of a vein, usually in the legs), in the Treatment group, with five thrombotic events (one DVT and four superficial thromboses) in the Control group.

  Pycnogenol Reduces Ankle Swelling (Edema): A 2005 study [20], which looked at the risk of edema (associated with increased risk of deep vein thrombosis) found that 100 mg of Pycnogenol (two capsules between 2 and 3 hours before flights with 250 ml. of water and two capsules 6 hours later with 250 ml. of water and one capsule the next day), significantly reduced the risk of ankle swelling (a sign of edema).

## RADIATION

Radiation exposure is cumulative. Whenever you fly, you are exposed to varying amounts of DNA-damaging radiation. Research[11] indicates that pilots and flight crew have around twice as much incidence of melanoma compared to the general population. A polar flight (polar routes are the most irradiated) going from Chicago to Beijing will expose the pilot to the equivalent of two chest x-rays. A frequent flyer who racks up 100,000 miles receives the equivalent of 20 chest x-rays.[12]

Most people think that the main radiation exposure during a flight comes from *cosmic rays*,[13] the radiation that comes from stars exploding in outer space, out beyond our solar system. Some cosmic rays come from our sun, and those are called *solar radiation*. At high altitudes, the air is thinner, which means there are fewer molecules to protect you from incoming cosmic rays—It is particularly strong during solar flares. A 7-hour flight from New York to Europe, will give a passenger about the same dose of radiation as a chest x-ray from cosmic or solar radiation. Short trips, like Atlanta to West Palm Beach, will produce about the same amount of radiation as a dental bitewing x-ray.

Today, our greatest radiation threat comes from radiation from nuclear accidents and detonations that is circulating in the jet stream where planes most often fly. We have voluminous radioisotopes pummeling out of Fukushima and other nuclear disasters or detonations, which continue to rise into the jet stream. Detonations in war zones, and which are used for military practice all add to the accumulating of radioactive pollution on the planet and in the atmosphere. I could not find any good statistics on exposure to this radiation while flying in the jet stream, but information on how the radiation travels in the jet streams and then falls out, is well documented.[25]

Although, the scanners in use today are reportedly "safe," recent research by Los Alamos has revealed that the TSA full body scanners are damaging to your DNA.[32]

- I "opt out" and get a pat down by security. Just tell the TSA agent before you go through the scanner that you want to "opt out." They will then ask you to wait. You might allow a few extra minutes for this process. In my opinion, it is worth it.


**SUGGESTIONS**

- Eating a plant-based diet, rich in fresh colorful foods is always helpful to your overall health.

Foods known to be radio protective are seaweeds and chlorella, found in Wild Water™.

- Be sure to bathe with soap and hot water and change into fresh clothes as soon as possible after the flight. Wash your clothes before wearing them again.

- Sauna and infrared sauna improve the elimination of radiation, toxins and heavy metals from the body. Plus, the immune system is more active when you raise your body temperature. Take a sauna, even daily, at least 20 minutes. Always follow your sauna with a cool shower, then warm shower and scrub with soap.   You can do 20 minutes in the sauna, shower, and then repeat for as much time as you have, up to an hour. Sauna can be dehydrating, so be sure to drink more water during and after you sauna.

- To a great extent, eating a diet rich in whole colorful foods brings antioxidants to the rescue for neutralizing the damaging effects of radiation.

- To avoid cosmic radiation and solar flares, take the red-eye or night flights as much as possible. There is significantly less solar radiation on night flights because the earth blocks some of the sun's radiation.

- I suggest sitting in the 5th to 10th row behind first class. In first class, sit in the second to the last row. Sitting in the aisle rather than by the window is better in terms of radiation exposure (although not in terms of pathogens).

## SUPPLEMENTS

- I use a couple of supplements to help with mitigating the effects of the radiation exposure. The most specific ones are Rad Zero™ and Energy Enhanced Alive Iodine™. The Rad Zero™ clears radiation from the body. The Energy Enhanced Alive Iodine™ saturates your thyroid with non-radioactive iodine, thus protecting your thyroid.

## JET LAG

One of the most well known problems connected to flying is jet lag. Flying through multiple time zones disrupts your normal circadian rhythm, and other natural biorhythms.

It is common to have difficulty concentrating, sleep disturbance, or brain fog from jet lag. You might find yourself falling asleep before dinner or wandering around wide-awake in the middle of the night feeling fatigued and disoriented.

## SUGGESTIONS

- Get on the local time zone as quickly as possible. If you arrive at night, go to bed right after your shower and sauna. If you arrive mid-day, try to stay up as late as you can. It is helpful to take naps while on a long flight but be mindful not to sleep before landing at night as you may then have trouble getting to sleep in the local time zone. Plan, so that you can acclimate to the time zone at your location.

- You can use a sleep aide like herbs from Gaia Herbs™, or something your doctor may recommend.

- On longer trips, plan a night layover to give your body a chance to adjust. If this isn't possible, it might be worth the extra money to fly first class. I try to save up my miles to use for upgrades on flights longer than 5-6 hours. When I fly between Hawaii and Florida, I like to plan an overnight in California to break up the 10-12 hour flight and get a good night's sleep.

- Wild Water™ is a wonderful aid for preventing jet lag. Take it before, during, and after your flight. This should not interfere with rest/sleep.

- "No Jet Lag™"14 is a homeopathic that helps you avoid the effects of jet lag.

- Get "grounded" after your flight. If possible, take off your shoes and stand or lie on the grass/earth for as long as you can, even up to an hour, especially if you can get some sun and breathe some fresh air at the same time.

You can purchase "anti-static mats" from Wal-Mart for under $20. These are similar to the Earthing™ mats that sell for over $100. You can use this mat after a flight under your head in bed or under your bare feet at your desk.

- I like to get a massage after I change clothes and shower. Massage can be helpful to relax, and to improve circulation and lymphatic return.

- Every morning, I do some stretching and deep breathing.

- Remember to drink adequate water!

## NAUSEA –Motion Sickness

Although motion sickness is not as common as it was before people were so accustomed to flying, it still occurs.

## SUGGESTIONS

- Take a moment to calm yourself and take some deep breaths. Think about someone you love. (I have a whole section with suggestions on anxiety that might help too.)

- Use organic ginger to calm your stomach. You can also purchase ginger tea crystals, which you can add to your water as a preventative, ginger hard candies, gummies or slices of fresh ginger root.

- If you don't like ginger you can use a homeopathic called NuxVomica. NuxVomica comes in small containers, as a liquid or small pills. If you are inclined to nausea, NuxVomica is a good remedy to keep on hand.

## ANXIETY

While I've never had "air-rage," I've experienced travel anxiety at times. This is normal. It is not uncommon to experience anxiety occasionally. If you're with someone, talking about it can help a lot. If it persists, you might want to seek professional help.

## SUGGESTIONS

- Bring something relaxing that you can listen to while flying. For a while, I listened to Louise Hay's *Love Your Body*™ on tape and imagined angels flying along and guiding the plane. Then, for awhile, I traveled with a small stuffed bear for comfort.

- Meditation, yoga, qigong, mindfulness and conscious breathing techniques are good ways to calm your self at anytime. If you are experiencing anxiety on a plane, start out by consciously calming yourself. Focus on your breath for a dozen or more breaths. Then, begin to breathe a little more deeply and slow it down a bit. Instead of thinking about anything else, just focus on your breath. You can even count. Breathe in for 4 counts and out for 8 counts. Roll your ankles and wrists and stretch a little.

- Think of something positive—those you love, your pet, or anything that will bring peace. After a while, make a list of 10-20 things you are grateful for. If you've been having a tough time, you can be thankful for even little things. Gratitude produces joy.

- Anti-anxiety and muscle relaxer herbal formulas are available if you are an anxious flyer or need to sleep. I like Gaia Herb formulas. Visit your local health food store or go online and try out an herbal or homeopathic formula. Ask for samples, as many companies do provide sample size packs. I've found that you might have to try a few to find the right one for you.

- I often use a little Bach Flower Rescue Remedy™ to help me relax. It comes in drops and in a spray.

- It is also possible for your doctor to prescribe an anti-anxiety medication to help you relax.


## HEARING LOSS:[15]

The occupational safety limit set by the National Institute for Occupational Safety and Health (NIOSH) is 88 decibels for four hours and 85 decibels for eight hours, while noise on a plane usually ranges between 95 and 105 decibels, and engine noise during take-off is usually upward of 115 decibels. The longer you are in the air, the greater the risk. The danger to your hearing is well known, but the disruption of the roar is undocumented. I think it is very tiring.

## SUGGESTIONS

* A noise-canceling headset will significantly protect your hearing.

   Even wearing ear plugs can provide some protection for your ears agains the damage.

* Pick a seat as far away from the engines as possible. If you are seated near the engine the risk is serious. Ask to be moved, or be sure to wear your noise-canceling headset.

# 5

## SPECIAL HEALTH CONCERNS

The World Health Organization says: Travelers with pre-existing health problems and those receiving medical care are more likely to be affected and should consult their doctor or a travel medicine clinic in good time before traveling.[26] On their site, they have a Medical Health Checklist for the traveler.[27] The WHO suggests that if you are on a medication listed as a controlled substance, you carry a copy of the prescription and enough medication for your entire journey.

**Babies and small children, pregnant women**, people with disabilities, and people with weakened immune systems all have special health needs. Take precautions recommended in this book and those recommended by your physician.

There is varying information about how flying affects a fetus. **If you are pregnant**, I hope you will use your own discretion, do your own research and check with your doctor or midwife before flying. The Center for Disease Control and Prevention is a good resource for more information on traveling and pregnancy. [29]

If you have **diabetes epilepsy** or other serious health conditions, travel with your ID card and necklace or bracelet. Carry your doctor's name and phone number with you in case of an emergency.

**If you are flying with a child or have a special health concern, like diabetes**, you may be able to bring larger sizes of liquids for nourishment or medication. Check before you fly.

Even before boarding a plane, **senior adults in particular may already be dehydrated** because their sense of thirst may be less acute, and may be compounded by illnesses like diabetes or dementia, or certain medications.

### Ear Pain during take off and descent

* Earplugs are helpful. There are few styles, and its up to you to choose what is the most comfortable and effective.

* Use the Valsalva technique for equalizing the pressure in your ears. You close your mouth and gently pinch your nostrils closed. Attempt to exhale gently. You should experience a light "popping" sensation in your ears. Repeat this step as needed during the ascent and descent portion of your airplane ride.

* Yawn repeatedly, stretch your jaw open during the ascent and descent before they start to hurt. This should help open your Eustachian tubes, which

will allow the pressure within your ears to equalize and prevent ear pain from occurring in the first place.

**Allergies:**

* If you have a life threatening allergy or a food allergy, travel with proper safety measures and identification in case of exposure. Have your ID bracelet or necklace outside your clothes where they can easily be seen.

**Breathing Problems:**

* If you have COPD or asthma, the slight decrease in oxygen and cabin pressure can lead to dizziness and vision impairment. You certainly want to wear an Air Purifying Face Mask with Activated Charcoal Filter. I would suggest also using the AirTamer™. FilterStream AirTamer personal air purifiers clean your air by removing airborne pollutants (e.g. viruses, bacteria, pollen, dust, etc.) from your personal space! I have a link for AirTamer on KatharineClarkRN.com.

* If you need supplemental oxygen, you can arrange it in advance with the airline for a fee. You might want to bring your own cannula or mask.

**Compromised Immune System:**

* If you are immune compromised, and/or seriously ill, you definitely want the particle mask with carbon filter. You may want to bring latex gloves

for the lavatory or even a disposable plastic raincoat for extra protection.

## Medication:

- Be sure to take more than enough of your prescription medication for your whole trip, in your carry-on bag.

- Ask your doctor if you need to change times or dosages during a long trip.

- Some medications we use in the USA are not available elsewhere.

- Some medications we use here are much less expensive in other countries. If you use medication, you might want to check out prices where you go. It is quite common for people to go to Canada and Mexico from the US to purchase medications at a better price.

## Scuba Diving:

Keep in mind it is dangerous to fly after certain activities, such as scuba diving. Wait 12 to 24 hours after diving before flying. Ask your diving teacher or a doctor for more information.

## Seat Belt:

Keep your seat belt on unless you are up walking. If there were a breach of cabin integrity, cabin contents will be sucked outside. Its safer to be wearing your seat belt.

# THE COMFORTABLE JETSETTER

I like to think of surrounding myself in a cocoon of comfort. I put on my hoodie, eye mask, N99 air purifier mask with charcoal filter and the Air Tamer air purifier, put on my headset, and set up my neck pillow support and I'm in my own little world.

Being comfortable during travel will help you feel better all around. This takes some forethought and planning. I have a list for the supplements and toiletries that I keep packed in a travel bag ready to go, below.

Be wary of the row of seats in front of the exit row, as these seats frequently will not recline. Also the last row of seats in the plane may not recline.

## SUGGESTIONS

- Wear comfortable clothing and shoes. Try to wear only natural fibers like cotton, linen, hemp or silk. These allow your body to "breathe". You will probably be walking more and sitting longer than usual. You might have a long and unexpected layover. Have clothes and shoes that do not bind you or cut off circulation when sitting.

- I use a soft foam cervical support. This is a soft foam that goes around your neck. It gently supports your head so it doesn't fall over if you go to sleep. This way I avoid needing a chiropractor after sleeping on a flight. It also helps keep my mouth closed while sleeping, so I am not drooling and drying out while mouth breathing.

## Qigong

### "If you want to live until 100, do qigong." Dr Oz

Qigong is a very pleasant way of being, which involves being mindful of breath, movement and purpose.

It is a self-healing, self-empowerment exercise. Research shows that when you do it, you get healthier. You can do qigong in more ways than one. You can even do it in your imagination.

I discovered qigong (chi kung) in 1991, while in Kauai. I read, "Transforming Stress Into Vitality" by Mantak Chia. That's when I started to practice. I did the practice of the Microcosmic Orbit and the Six Healing Sounds while lying in bed. I used my imagination. I did experience benefits from this after awhile. So eventually, I found more books, and started doing more movement.

You probably have local teachers and you can certainly go online to learn more. There are many books available. Gaiam has Daisy Lee and Francesco Garipolli on DVD. They are my teachers.

### FIRST CLASS

If you're going to be in the air for more than five or six hours, it is worth considering investing in business or first class. While you don't reduce your health risks, you do increase your comfort. Be sure to ask the airline about the first class seats, space, and amenities. Some first class cabins sport fully flat sleeping arrangements and I think this is worth buying if you're flying 8-10 hours and overnight.

A good night's rest is worth more than the cost, if you can afford it. (Many credit cards now offer frequent flyer miles.)

I've been disappointed when the seats did not recline on a red eye. I once used 200,000 miles for a first class overnight flight from Hawaii to LA. When I boarded, I found the seats hardly reclined at all. There were no pillows or blankets, and the flight was miserable. Not only was I uncomfortable, but I was angry, too. I complained to the airline again and again, until I finally got someone who helped me get a much better first class service back to Hawaii.

## CARRY ON CHECKLIST

Here's a checklist of items you may want to keep in your carry on kit. I will update this and give you my preferred sources, on my site: KatharineClarkRN.com.

Your general level of health, and the frequency with which you fly, will influence how many precautions you choose to take. I do not use all the precautions or solutions, I've mentioned. As I have said, a strong immune system is your best defense. Staying well hydrated is the best way to support your health, in my experience. Take the suggestions that appeal to you, or work for you, or address your particular concerns, and leave the rest.

- Sanitizer gel, wipes and/or sprays (I like Thieves Spray from Young Living)

- If needed, bring lip balm, moisturizer, eye drops and nasal spray from food grade, non-toxic ingredients.

- Air Purifier (Link on KatharineClarkRN.com to AirTamer)

- Air Purifying Face Mask with activated carbon filter (Organic N99 mask from VogMask.com I have a coupon on KatharineClarkRN.com) or the Charcoal Cellulose Nose Filters.

- Water filter (See Link on KatharineClarkRN.com)

- Noise canceling headsets are important for frequent flyers. Use ear plugs at the least.

- I like to listen to books on tape, but sometimes I just listen to subliminal music as white noise to block out the crying kids, rude neighbors, or boring chatterboxes.

- Medications, if you need them

- Breath freshener (Use one that is mint oil in honey rather than gum or mints with sugar or artificial flavors, sweeteners and color)

- Stool softener or laxative (AloeLax™ or OxyMag™ are my favorites)

- Water and drink enhancements. (See list)

- Personal blanket, if needed for warmth or rolled up behind you to support your lumbar area. Remember unless the airline blanket is in sealed plastic, it is unclean.

- Neck support: a firm foam cervical collar. VIP for me!

- Blackout eye mask for when you sleep, if you choose.

- Slippers, washable, if you need to take off tight shoes. Keep these in a baggie and wash both after the flight.

- Hoodie to keep my hair off the seat. This takes the place of a personal blanket for me. I wear layers and dress warmly because I'm cold natured. I like a natural fiber hoodie, cotton, bamboo, hemp or silk.

- Supplements (see list)

- Remedies (see list)

## My Travel bag

I always take a carry-on with wheels on which, I can rest my coat, purse, or service animal on top when I'm in the rest room or traveling the terminal traffic. It is worth investing in a good quality, lightweight roll aboard bag with very good wheels that move in all directions easily.

Remember, in your carry on which goes through security, all liquids must be in 3.4 ounce (100ml) **bottle** or less (by volume) inside 1 quart-sized, clear, plastic, zip-top bag; 1 baggie per passenger placed in screening bin at security.[30] You can fit a few of the 100ml bottles into the baggie.

- I suggest keeping a travel bag of essentials ready to go with travel size or sample size toiletries, remedies, supplements, jewelry, color coordinated layerable clothes and a few small gift items like essential oils in a gift bag with a blank gift card.

- You can purchase empty bottles, not more than 100ml size, to fill with your own goodies. Be sure to label them with an indelible marker. I collect samples of soap, shampoo, conditioner, and lotions, at the health food store and take them with me during travel.

- I've collected a wrinkle-free, color-coordinated, easy-to-layer, all natural fiber wardrobe for travel. I like to have pockets in my clothes. This helps keep things handy, and it provides a place to stash the sanitizer and rubber gloves!

- I like to wear a hoodie during the flight. I pull the hood up over my head so my hair doesn't touch the seat or other surfaces.

- I keep a few extra baggies in my suitcase zipper pocket to organize items that I might acquire while traveling. They come in handy for organizing or for taking a day's supply of supplements with me.

- Slippers: If you want to slip off your shoes on the plane, bring a pair of waterproof slippers in a plastic bag. You don't want to go into the lavatory barefooted, or in socks. After the flight, put those slippers back into the plastic bag and be sure to wash them and the bag!

- Neck Support: If you plan on napping, a handy item to use during your flight is a good neck support. I suggest a <u>foam cervical collar</u> that helps support your neck, keeping it straight and unstressed. This type of collar keeps your mouth closed, helps you breathe through your nose and prevents a stiff neck by keeping your head supported if you fall asleep.

- I have a cute bag where I keep a clean Air Purifying Face Mask with activated carbon filter,

    My AirTamer

    Neck Support

    Noise Canceling Headset

    Lip balm & Moisturizers

    Thieves spray and wipes.

- I have another cute bag with my supplements and water treatments for use during the flight(s).

- If you are cold natured, it is best to wear layers, and a hat and socks. Bring your own blanket if you want. You might invest in a thin thermal coverlet that you keep in your carry-on in a baggie. You do need to wash these after each use.

A report by *The Wall Street Journal*[16] claimed that airlines washed their blankets only every five to 30 days. Nowadays, blankets are often for sale on the plane rather than free. Only use an airline blanket if it is sealed in a plastic bag.

## SUPPLEMENTS

Here are some helpful nutrients and supplements for flying safely that I bring and use on every trip. I am not making claims or guarantees for the effectiveness of these products for your use. I'm simply sharing products that I have used. Please use your own judgment and check with your physicians if you have any concerns or considerations about using any of these products. See updates on KatharineClarkRN.com.

Remember, your overall health and immunity is the most important way to thrive as a jetsetter. What you do every day is going to build your health or break it down. So, hopefully you will choose to eat a diet high in fresh organic fruits and vegetables and limit processed food, sugar and acidifying beverages (soda, bottled juice, coffee).

I've been using most of these supplements for years. You many notice that I've recommended many of them for multiple uses. I've chosen them because they are of the highest quality, and plant-based. They are mostly foods that are supportive to your overall health with benefits specific to the jetsetter.

**Nutrition:** I like to take these dried concentrated organic whole foods that are often effective in small amounts. I'll share the ones I use and you will make your own choices.

- Essentials™ and Wild Essentials™ (Wild-SuperFood.com). These are packets that contain enzymes and probiotics with other nutrient foods. Wild Water™, Wild Earth™, and Wild Forest™ (a combination of tonic mushrooms) are found in Wild Essentials™ along with enzymes and probiotics. They are excellent, convenient, and cheaper than buying the same quality separately. Wild Water will help you to regulate the time change. (Wild-SuperFood.com check out the research, and the product page.)

- Food based digestive enzymes to support your digestive system. Take these when you eat and for sure every morning to support your immune system and healthy digestion. (Check product page WildAlgaeLove.com)

- Probiotics to support immunity and healthy gut flora. Since air travel is known to damage your friendly flora, it makes sense to take probiotics.

Probiotics can also help you stay regular, and avoid constipation and diarrhea. (Look for Spectrabiotic on WildAlgaeLove.com)

- For Vitamin C: I like to take an organic whole foods product. Often, Camu Camu powder and/or Rosehips powder are included. You can find a variety of vitamin C products. Vitamin C has been found to be immune enhancing, as well as antibacterial, antiviral, and anti-fungal. (MountainRoseHerbs.com, HealthForce and Vital Synergy have good organic whole food vitamin C.)

**Hydration**

To help me better absorb the water I'm drinking, and provide minerals to my body, I use:

- I use Scalar Salts™. I keep this in a small container in my travel bag. I add 1/8 teaspoon to every 8 ounces of water.

  You can use other salt, sea salt, pink salt, but I do not recommend iodized table salt. You want a salt that comes from nature, and is made up of many minerals. (SelinaNaturally.com has good salt products)

  If you have high blood pressure or another condition affecting your salt requirements you must follow your doctors protocol for salt consumption

Other products that make water more absorbable:

- Mega Hydrate™

- Crystal Energy Tincture™

- A squirt of Lemon. If you have nothing else, you can usually get lemon from the galley or in a café along the way.

- BioAgile has many benefits including maximizing brain health, cellular performance and improving hydration. The bottles are small enough to fit a few into your carry on baggie of liquids. Available from LivingLightFood.com

**Nutritious Drink Enhancers**

- Packets of Oxylent™, a fizzing multivitamin powder comes in 3 flavors.[31]

- Packet of Dried Miso Soup

**Radiation Protection and Detox:**

Rad Zero™, Active Enhanced Alive Iodine™, Crystal Clinoptilolite™ are on my KatharineClarkRN.com under shopping.

Wild Essential™ from Wild-SuperFood.com have properties which might assist your body in elimination of radiation. They are called: radioprotective.

## Cold/Flu/Diarrhea Remedies

- Oscillococcinum has a remedy for Flu and one for Cold. Take them as soon as you suspect you are getting the cold or flu, or if you are exposed to someone with the cold or flu. Order online or pick up in the health food store.

- Diarrhea remedy: If you do develop diarrhea, remember to stay hydrated, and eat only bland food. Some say oatmeal, or banana for instance. Chia or flax seed powder can help solidify your stool. Check out a homeopathic remedy that you can carry with you or something your physician recommends. If diarrhea lasts more than a few days, you want to be checked out by a doctor for parasites or other complications.

There are many other products and supplements that are helpful. I'm listing the ones that I currently use. I welcome your comments and suggestions at KatharineClarkRN.com.

### Research Your Destination:

Its great to research the traffic flow, parking, and layout of the terminals you'll be traveling in. You can call in advance to see if there are juice bars, organic foods, or water purifiers available. (In third world countries you may want only cooked food, unless you know the source and cleanliness of produce for salads, smoothies and juices.)

I like to research my destination in advance to find healthy food, and places to workout, do yoga or go for a walk, and unwind.

Once, when I was in Bangalore, India, there was a sugar cane juice stand that I loved to frequent. One day, thinking that the juice maker did not understand English, I commented to my companion on how many flies there were around the counter. The proprietor immediately grabbed the washcloth from the bucket of water where he washed the empty glasses. Then he doused it with DDT from can and wiped down the counter and machine, before dropping the cloth back into the bucket of dish wash water. Needless to say, I did not go there for juice again. Be aware that third world countries have different standards and laws that may affect the safety of food and drink.

## Food

Food is important to me, so I like to scout out ahead of time where I can get organic food and check for restaurants of my liking. I search online for "organic food" or "farm to table' on www.ecosia.org.

Be sure to read the description of the restaurant. Often Thai restaurants and sushi bars will show up in a search for organic or raw food, but they might not be what you're looking for, meaning they have organic meat and raw fish.

If you're in a rush, you can call ahead and order your food to be waiting when you arrive, or to grab and go.

UberEats or another local food taxi is one way to get your food delivered. Whole Foods Markets may also deliver.

## Bonus Travel Suggestions

- Go to Busy Restaurants especially in third world countries: The most likely way you'll get sick is from food or water. Go to a busy place where lots of people are eating. If the place is deserted, just walk on by. You can research restaurants and grocery stores before you go.

- Avoid Buffets: Buffets are suspect places to eat. Be ware and choose a busy restaurant when possible. You don't ever touch your plate with the serving utensil. If you do, you risk contaminating the dish with the saliva from your used plate. When you are at a buffet, you are supposed to get a clean plate when you go back for seconds.

- Be aware: When in third world countries, you want to eat only cooked food and beverages from unopened bottles, unless you are certain of the safety of raw food and beverages. Even boiling is inadequate to make water safe. Hot beverages like tea, cocoa and coffee may not have been boiled.

Here are helpful online sites to find good food:

- www.HappyCow.net
- www.OrganicHighways.com

- www.EatWellGuide.org/localguide

- www.vrg.org

- www.rawfoodplanet.com

- www.LocalHarvest.org/restaurants You can also check for farmer's markets and tailgate markets here.

- www.sunfoodtraveler.com

- Meetup.com can connect you with like-minded people. Enter the zip code of your destination and plan ahead if you want to connect. When you find a meet-up that resonates, check their "file" section to see if there is a list of local resources, cafes, stores, groceries, markets, or restaurants of interest.

Sources for other products I've mentioned will be updated on my website: KatharineClarkRN.com

## Summary of Basic Recommendations

I have many links on KatharineClarkRN.com under freebies and shopping tabs as sources and resources. I am updating that often. I applogize in advance that I do not have just one link to order everything, yet.

1. Stay hydrated. Chronic dehydration is common. Some people are not aware when they are dehydrated. There really is no replacement for drinking water. Being hydrated is essential for optimal health on the ground and in the sky.

2. Be mindful. Keep your stress level down. Allow plenty of time for yourself. Don't sweat the small stuff.

3. Practice good hygiene. Keep your hands away from your face. Wash your hands well. Use paper towel to open doors to exit tolit.

4. Daily, eat a variety of fresh colorful whole foods. Sprouts are at the top of my list for fresh vegetables. Eat naturally, refrigerated fermented foods daily, like kimchi, or sauerkraut to support your microbiome.

5. Although the particle filter mask (N99) with the charcoal filter looks like Darth Vader, it is effective for eliminating your exposure to airborn pathogens and toxins. (Organic one at VogMask.com). You can also use nasal filters. (gadgetsgo.com)

6. After your flight, shower yourself as soon as possible. Do not wear the same clothes from the flight until you wash them too!

7. Consume whole food based supplements including medicinal mushrooms, and edible algae with digestive enzymes and probiotics. I eat these daily. I list many in the supplements section.

## So, when in the airport terminal... what do you eat?

1. Fresh Fruits, whole or pre-cut. (Pre-cut usually has a preservative)

2. The packaged salads, you can grab and go

3. Fresh oatmeal, chia pudding, or acai bowl/

Do the best you can. Its better to eat light before you fly, and save the splurge for your first meal at your destination. I also bring digestive enzymes. These support your digestion and help me a lot, to avoid indigestion, gas, bloating, fatigue and constipation.

## What to bring: (If you want to bring snacks for the trip.)

1. My favorite is nori sheets. They're lightweight, thin, pack well, last awhile, and you can use them to wrap up the sprouts and avocado you bring in a baggie. Bring a salad in a baggie. You can add

your sprouts to a salad that you get in the terminal, or on board.

2. Fresh ripe juicy fruit, apple, banana, pears, grapes, or citrus, etc.

3. An avocado which goes nicely in the nori with the salad.

4. Dried berries, fruits and raw nuts travel well, but you will want to have more water when you eat dried foods.

5. Crudités: sticks of celery, carrot, jicima, red pepper, etc. (You can often find a prepackaged box like this at the grocery or in the terminal in the grab and go section.)

6. Single serving packs of nut butter; you can find organic almond, hazelnut, cashew or sunflower. These go nicely with fruit or crudités.

7. Good organic dark chocolates!

8. You may get through security with a chia pudding or oatmeal in a baggie. Flatten the baggie and put it between some papers or along the edge of your suitcase. I've used this method to get through security quite a few times, and have never been stopped, yet!

**What to avoid**

1. Overly sweet or caffeinated, carbonated, dairy or alcoholic beverages.

2. Complex meals with many different items. If you opt for a burger, skip the coke and fries. If you opt for the fries with catsup, skip the coffee and sandwich. The less complex, the easier for your body to digest, absorb and eliminate.

3. Laboratory made fake sugar found in sugar-free items like: Aspartame, Splenda, artifical and natural flavors, artifical colors, chemical preservatives, etc. (Carry your own Stevia if possible. Stevia, and honey are the better sweeteners.)

4 Chewing gum. Chewing causes your digestive tract to activate as if food is coming. You body is set to digest but no food is coming so this can have negative effects that may or may not be or become significant.

While gum is popular, its difficult to find one that is organic and made with real ingredients as opposed to made in a lab. You can find better gum at the health food store. Gum made with maple syrup instead of corn syrup, for instance.

# ABOUT THE AUTHOR

Katharine Clark, RN, CHHC, is an author, speaker, coach and registered nurse specializing in nutrition and wellness lifestyle education. She uses a whole being, integrative approach to wellness, nurturing clients into health on the emotional, spiritual, mental, and physical levels by helping them find their own inner knowing, inspiration and motivation to live a vibrant life. She is available for private duty, personal coaching, and speaking engagements.

For more information, go to www.KatharineClarkRN.com.

# ENDNOTES

[1] Gavish I, Brenner B. Air travel and the Risk of Thromboembolism, *Intern Emerg Med* 2011 Apr: Apr: 6(2): 113-6

[2] http://www.cieh.org/library/Knowledge/Public_health/JEHR/ JEHRVol3lss1CommonColdAircraft.pdf

[3] https://www.mayoclinic.org/diseases-conditions/dehydration/ symptoms-causes/syc-20354086

[4] http://www.dailymail.co.uk/health/article-4563050/Change-time-eat-overcome-jet-lag.html

[5] https://lifehacker.com/beat-jet-lag-by-eating-meals-on-local-time-before-you-t-1791989410

[6] http://ocm.auburn.edu/newsroom/featured_story/ airliner.html#.WkVXXyPMwe0

[7] https://www.travelmath.com/feature/airline-hygiene-exposed/

[8] Gavish I. Brenner B. Air travel and the Risk of Thromboembolism, *Intern Emerg Med* 2011 Apr: 6 (2):113-6.

[9] Blood Clots and travel: What You Need to Know. Center for Disease Control and Prevention, https://www.cdc.gov/ncbddd/ dvt/travel.html

[10] Effect of a novel workstation device on promoting non-exercise activity thermogenesis (NEAT): Horswill, Craig A. | Scott, Haley M. | Voorhees, Daniel M. Affiliations: Department of Kinesiology and Nutrition, University of Illinois at Chicago, IL; Prevention and Wellness Center, Northwest Community Hospital, Arlington Heights, IL

[11] https://jamanetwork.com/journals/jamadermatology/fullarticle/ 1899248

[13] https://science.nasa.gov/science-news/science-at-nasa/2013/ 25oct_aviationswx/

[13]https://www.hindawi.com/journals/ab/2014/198609/

[14] http://www.nojetlag.com

[15]http://www.dailymail.co.uk/travel/travel_news/
article-2852166/A-complete-guide-flying-affects-health-combat-
it.html#ixzz54D12fxcC
[18]http://edition.cnn.com/2010/TRAVEL/12/22/
bt.germs.breed.on.plane/
[20] "© How Pine Bark Extract Could Save Air Travelers
Lives"[May 11th 2014] GreenMedInfo LLC. This work is
reproduced and distributed with the permission
of GreenMedInfo LLC. Want to learn more from GreenMedInfo?
Sign up for the newsletter here http://www.greenmedinfo.com/
greenmed/newsletter"
[21]http://www.dailymail.co.uk/travel/travel_news/article-3450962/
Aerotoxic-syndrome-documentary-claims-passengers-crew-
inhaling-poisonous-fumes.html#ixzz55cQlnydQ
[22]https://beatcancer.org/blog-posts/flying-and-aerotoxic-
syndrome
[23]https://www.livescience.com/13878-health-hazards-air-
travel.html
[24] "SAFE SOCKS: WHAT YOUR MOTHER NEVER TOLD
YOU" https://opedge.com/Articles/ViewArticle/
2016-10-26/2016-11_03
[25]"Live Jet Stream Wind Map Of World Radiation Fallout USA"
http://miami-water.com/blog/3305/live-jet-stream-wind-map-of-
world-radiation-fallout-usa/
[26] http://www.who.int/ith/mode_of_travel/air_travel/en/
[27]http://www.who.int/ith/precautions/ITH_checklist.pdf?ua=1
[28]https://www.healthline.com/health-news/real-airplane-health-
dangers-052414#3
[29]https://wwwnc.cdc.gov/travel/yellowbook/2018/advising-
travelers-with-specific-needs/pregnant-travelers
[30]https://www.dhs.gov/how-do-i/learn-what-i-can-bring-plane
[31]http://www.oxylent.com/know-whats-water-enhancer/
[32] http://humansarefree.com/2017/02/los-alamos-study-finds-
airport-scanners.html
[33]https://www.telegraph.co.uk/travel/news/travel-advice-what-
happens-to-your-body-on-a-flight-travel-health/
[34]https://www.smartertravel.com/2017/06/19/avoiding-airplane-

Made in the USA
Columbia, SC
19 May 2020